Easy Home Cooking

OLD-FASHIONED
Holidays

Publications International, Ltd.

Favorite Brand Name Recipes at www.fbnr.com

Microwave Cooking: Microwave ovens vary in wattage. Use the cooking times as guidelines and check for doneness before adding more time.

Preparation/Cooking Times: Preparation times are based on the approximate amount of time required to assemble the recipe before cooking, baking, chilling or serving. These times include preparation steps such as measuring, chopping and mixing. The fact that some preparations and cooking can be done simultaneously is taken into account. Preparation of optional ingredients and serving suggestions is not included.

CONTENTS

KITCHEN SENSE

From Thanksgiving Eve through New Year's Day—the holiday season is certainly a busy time of year. Grocery shopping, wrapping presents, office and kids' parties, holiday decorating and baking—the list goes on and on.

Take the stress out of holiday planning this year and make the most of this joyful season.

Have the Mall to Yourself

Shop for gifts and groceries during the week at off-peak hours. Sales people are less taxed and will have more time to help you. Use the weekends for baking and household chores.

HOLIDAY SHOPPERS AHEAD

'Tis the Season to Be Baking

Bring back the old-fashioned joy of cookie baking to your holidays this year by following these useful tips.

• If holiday baking is a family event, choose recipes that are easy enough for the kids to help with. Have plenty of decorations on hand and let their creativity flow.

• To guarantee freshness, keep purchased dry goods unopened in their original packaging until you are ready to use them.

• Before you begin, double check the recipe to make sure you have all the necessary ingredients and equipment called for.

• Measure all the ingredients accurately and assemble them in the order they are called for in the recipe.

• Follow recipe directions and baking times exactly. Check for doneness using the test given in the recipe.

• Remove butter and cream cheese from the refrigerator to soften, if necessary.

Write It Down!

Make a large poster-board calendar and hang it on the wall. Decorate it with a holiday theme. Start with Thanksgiving Day and end with New Year's Day 2000. Fill in the dates that you already have plans for. As invitations come in and party plans are finalized, add these dates to your calendar. Use different colored markers for kids' parties, office parties and family gatherings.

Help for Busy Elves

Is the thought of preparing Christmas dinner filling you with yuletide dread? Take a shortcut this year by purchasing the main dish. Many large supermarkets now sell roasted turkeys for the holidays. Just heat and serve with your favorite homemade side dishes and desserts. Remember to order in advance.

LET THEM WRAP IT

Many charitable organizations offer gift wrapping services at shopping malls during the holidays, and for a nominal fee most department stores provide this service as well.

Healthy Holidays are Happy Holidays

Don't push yourself too hard. Do a little every day and enjoy this wonderful season.

HOLIDAY GATHERINGS

Festive Yule Loaf

2¾ cups all-purpose flour,
   divided
⅓ cup sugar
1 teaspoon salt
1 package active dry yeast
1 cup milk
½ cup butter or margarine
1 egg
½ cup golden raisins
½ cup chopped candied red
   and green cherries
½ cup chopped pecans
   Vanilla Glaze (recipe
   follows, optional)

Combine 1½ cups flour, sugar, salt and yeast in large bowl. Heat milk and butter over medium heat until very warm (120° to 130°F). Gradually stir into flour mixture. Add egg. Mix with electric mixer on low speed 1 minute. Beat on high speed 3 minutes, scraping sides of bowl frequently. Toss raisins, cherries and pecans with ¼ cup flour in small bowl; stir into yeast mixture. Stir in enough of remaining 1 cup flour to make a soft dough. Turn out onto lightly floured surface. Knead about 10 minutes or until smooth and elastic. Place in greased bowl; turn to grease top of dough. Cover with towel. Let rise in warm, draft-free place about 1 hour or until double in volume.

Punch dough down. Divide in half. Roll out each half on lightly floured surface to form 8-inch circle. Fold in half; press only folded edge firmly. Place on ungreased cookie sheet. Cover with towel. Let rise in warm, draft-free place about 30 minutes or until double in volume.

Preheat oven to 375°F. Bake 20 to 25 minutes until golden brown. Remove from cookie sheet and cool completely on wire rack. Frost with Vanilla Glaze, if desired. Store in airtight containers.

Makes 2 loaves

Vanilla Glaze: Combine 1 cup sifted powdered sugar, 4 to 5 teaspoons light cream or half-and-half and ½ teaspoon vanilla extract in small bowl; stir until smooth.

Cranberry-Apple Chutney

1¼ cups granulated sugar
½ cup water
1 package (12 ounces) fresh
   or frozen cranberries
   (about 3½ cups)
2 medium Granny Smith
   apples, cut into ¼-inch
   pieces (about 2 cups)
1 medium onion, chopped
½ cup golden raisins
½ cup packed light brown
   sugar
¼ cup cider vinegar
1 teaspoon ground ginger
1 teaspoon ground cinnamon
⅛ teaspoon ground allspice
⅛ teaspoon ground cloves
½ cup walnuts or pecans,
   toasted and chopped
   (optional)

Combine granulated sugar and water in heavy 2-quart saucepan. Bring to a boil over high heat. Boil gently 3 minutes. Add cranberries, apples, onion, raisins, brown sugar, vinegar, ginger, cinnamon, allspice and cloves.

Bring to a boil over high heat. Reduce heat to medium. Simmer, uncovered, 20 to 25 minutes or until mixture is very thick, stirring occasionally. Cool; stir in walnuts, if desired. Cover and refrigerate up to 2 weeks before serving.

*Makes about 3½ cups
without walnuts or
4 cups with walnuts*

Make Ahead Tip

This chutney keeps well and may be prepared 2 weeks ahead of the party. Store the chutney in the refrigerator until you are ready to serve it.

Cranberry-Apple Chutney

Pesto Cheese Wreath

Parsley-Basil Pesto (recipe follows)
3 packages (8 ounces each) cream cheese, softened
½ cup mayonnaise
¼ cup whipping cream or half-and-half
1 teaspoon sugar
1 teaspoon onion salt
⅓ cup chopped roasted red peppers* or pimiento, drained
Pimiento strips and Italian flat leaf parsley leaves (optional)
Assorted crackers and cut-up vegetables

* Look for roasted red peppers packed in cans or jars in the Italian food section of the supermarket.

Prepare Parsley-Basil Pesto; set aside. Beat cream cheese and mayonnaise in medium bowl until smooth; beat in cream, sugar and onion salt.

Line 5-cup ring mold with plastic wrap. Spoon half of cheese mixture into prepared mold; spread evenly. Spread Parsley-Basil Pesto evenly over cheese mixture; top with chopped red peppers. Spoon remaining cheese mixture over peppers; spread evenly. Cover; refrigerate until cheese mixture is firm, 8 hours or overnight.

Uncover mold; invert onto serving plate. Carefully remove plastic wrap. Smooth top and sides of wreath with spatula. Garnish with pimiento strips and parsley leaves, if desired. Serve with assorted crackers and vegetables.

Makes 16 to 24 appetizer servings

PARSLEY-BASIL PESTO
2 cups fresh parsley leaves
¼ cup pine nuts or slivered almonds
2 tablespoons grated Parmesan cheese
2 cloves garlic, peeled
1 tablespoon dried basil leaves, crushed
¼ teaspoon salt
2 tablespoons olive or vegetable oil

Process all ingredients except oil in food processor or blender until finely chopped. With machine running, add oil gradually, processing until mixture is smooth.

Makes about ½ cup

Little Christmas Pizzas

⏸⏸⏸

⅓ cup olive oil
1 tablespoon **TABASCO®** brand Pepper Sauce
2 large cloves garlic, minced
1 teaspoon dried rosemary, crushed
1 (16-ounce) package hot roll mix with yeast packet
1¼ cups hot water*
Flour

TOPPINGS

1 large tomato, diced
¼ cup crumbled goat cheese
2 tablespoons chopped fresh parsley
½ cup shredded mozzarella cheese
½ cup pitted green olives
⅓ cup roasted red pepper strips
½ cup chopped artichoke hearts
½ cup cherry tomatoes, sliced into wedges
⅓ cup sliced green onions

Check hot roll mix package directions for temperature of water.

Combine olive oil, TABASCO® Sauce, garlic and rosemary in small bowl. Combine hot roll mix, yeast packet, hot water and 2 tablespoons TABASCO® mixture in large bowl; stir until dough pulls away from side of bowl. Turn dough onto lightly floured surface; shape dough into a ball. Knead until smooth, adding additional flour as necessary.

Preheat oven to 425°F. Cut dough into quarters; cut each quarter into 10 equal pieces. Roll each piece into a ball. On large cookie sheet, press each ball into 2-inch round. Brush each with remaining TABASCO® Sauce mixture. Arrange approximately 2 teaspoons toppings on each dough round. Bake 12 minutes or until dough is lightly browned and puffed.

Makes 40 appetizer servings

Christmas Ribbon

2 packages (4-serving size each) or 1 package (8-serving size) JELL-O® Brand Strawberry Flavor Gelatin Dessert
5 cups boiling water, divided
⅔ cup BREAKSTONE'S® or KNUDSEN® Sour Cream or BREYERS® Plain or Vanilla Lowfat Yogurt, divided
2 packages (4-serving size each) or 1 package (8-serving size) JELL-O® Brand Lime Flavor Gelatin Dessert

Dissolve strawberry flavor gelatin in 2½ cups of the boiling water. Pour 1½ cups gelatin into 6-cup ring mold. Chill until set but not firm, about 30 minutes. Chill remaining gelatin in bowl until slightly thickened; gradually blend in ⅓ cup of the sour cream. Spoon over gelatin in mold. Chill until set but not firm, about 15 minutes.

Repeat with lime flavor gelatin, using remaining 2½ cups boiling water and ⅓ cup sour cream. Chill dissolved gelatin before measuring and pouring into mold. Chill at least 2 hours. Unmold.

Makes 12 servings

Prep Time: 30 minutes
Chill Time: 3 hours

Sweet Potato Soufflé

3 eggs, separated
¾ cup sugar
1¼ cups mashed sweet potatoes, fresh or canned
1 cup chopped walnuts, divided
Sugar
Whipped cream (optional)

Preheat oven to 350°F.

Beat egg yolks in large bowl until frothy. Gradually add sugar; beat until lemon colored. Add sweet potatoes and ½ of walnuts; beat until blended.

Beat egg whites in separate bowl until stiff peaks form; fold into sweet potato mixture. Turn into buttered and lightly sugared soufflé dish. Sprinkle remaining walnuts on top. Dust with sugar. Bake 15 minutes. Serve immediately with whipped cream, if desired. *Makes 6 servings*

Favorite recipe from **Walnut Marketing Board**

Holiday Appetizer Quiche

▊ ▊ ▊

CRUST
  2 cups all-purpose flour
  1 teaspoon salt
  ¾ cup Butter Flavor*
    CRISCO® Stick or ¾ cup
    Butter Flavor CRISCO®
    all-vegetable shortening
  5 tablespoons cold water

FILLING
  2 cups (8 ounces) shredded
    Swiss cheese
  ⅔ cup chopped ham,
    crumbled cooked
    sausage, diced
    pepperoni or crumbled
    cooked bacon
  ¾ cup thinly sliced green
    onions (including tops)
  ¼ cup snipped fresh parsley
  1 jar (4 ounces) diced
    pimientos, well drained
  5 eggs
  1 cup whipping cream
  1 cup half-and-half
  1 teaspoon salt
  ¼ teaspoon pepper

Butter Flavor Crisco is artificially flavored.

1. Heat oven to 400°F.

2. For crust, combine flour and salt in medium bowl. Cut in ¾ cup shortening using pastry blender (or 2 knives) until all flour is blended in to form pea-size chunks. Sprinkle with water, 1 tablespoon at a time. Toss lightly with fork until dough forms ball.

3. Roll out dough to fit 15×10-inch jelly-roll pan. Place dough in greased pan, folding edges under. Flute edges. Prick crust with fork.

4. For filling, sprinkle cheese, ham, onions, parsley and pimientos evenly over crust. Beat eggs, cream, half-and-half, salt and pepper in medium bowl. Pour over filled crust.

5. Bake at 400°F for 25 to 30 minutes or until set. Cool 5 to 10 minutes. Cut into 2×1½-inch pieces. Serve warm.

Makes about 50 appetizers

Note: Crust may bubble during baking and need to be pricked with fork again.

Early American Pumpkin Pie

1½ cups cooked pumpkin,
 canned or fresh
1 cup whole or 2% milk
2 eggs, beaten
1 cup sugar
1 tablespoon butter or
 margarine, melted
½ teaspoon ground cinnamon
¼ teaspoon salt
¼ teaspoon ground ginger
¼ teaspoon ground nutmeg
1 (9-inch) unbaked pie shell
 Sweetened whipped cream
 or whipped topping
 (optional)
 Fresh currants (optional)

Preheat oven to 425°F.
Combine all ingredients except
pie shell, cream and currants
in large bowl; blend well. Pour
into pie shell. Bake 45 to 50
minutes or until knife inserted
into filling comes out clean.
Cool completely. Serve with
whipped cream and garnish
with currants, if desired.
Refrigerate leftovers.

Makes 6 to 8 servings

Favorite recipe from
Bob Evans®

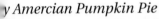
y Amercian Pumpkin Pie

Seasonal Sides

Wild Rice with Dried Apricots and Cranberries

▌▌▌

½ cup uncooked wild rice, rinsed and drained
3 cups chicken broth, divided
1 cup apple juice
¾ cup uncooked long-grain white rice
½ cup golden raisins
½ cup chopped dried apricots
½ cup dried cranberries
2 tablespoons butter
¾ cup chopped onion
½ cup coarsely chopped pecans
⅓ cup chopped fresh parsley

1. Combine wild rice, 1½ cups chicken broth and apple juice in 2-quart saucepan. Bring to a boil over medium-high heat. Reduce heat to low; simmer, covered, about 1 hour or until rice is tender. Drain; set aside.

2. Combine white rice and remaining 1½ cups broth in separate 2-quart saucepan. Bring to a boil over medium-high heat. Reduce heat to low; simmer, covered, 12 to 15 minutes.

3. Stir in raisins, apricots and cranberries; simmer 5 minutes or until rice is tender and fluffy and liquid is absorbed. Remove from heat. Let stand, covered, 5 minutes or until fruit is tender; set aside.

4. Melt butter in large skillet over medium heat. Add onion; cook and stir 5 to 6 minutes or until tender. Stir in pecans. Cook and stir 2 minutes.

5. Add wild rice and white rice mixtures to skillet. Stir in parsley; cook and stir over medium heat about 2 minutes or until heated through. Garnish with fresh thyme, orange slices and whole cranberries, if desired.

Makes 6 to 8 servings

Golden Apples and Yams

■ ■ ■

2 large yams or sweet
  potatoes
2 Washington Golden
  Delicious apples, cored
  and sliced crosswise into
  rings
¼ cup firmly packed brown
  sugar
1 teaspoon cornstarch
⅛ teaspoon ground cloves
½ cup orange juice
2 tablespoons chopped
  pecans or walnuts

Heat oven to 400°F. Bake yams 50 minutes or until soft but still hold their shape. Let yams cool enough to handle. *Reduce oven to 350°F.*

Peel and slice yams crosswise. In shallow 1-quart baking dish, alternate apple rings and yam slices, overlapping edges slightly. In small saucepan, combine sugar, cornstarch and cloves; stir in orange juice and mix well. Heat orange juice mixture over medium heat, stirring, until thickened; pour over apples and yams. Sprinkle with nuts; bake 20 minutes or until apples and yams are tender. *Makes 6 servings*

Favorite recipe from
**Washington Apple
Commission**

Pepperidge Farm® Sausage Corn Bread Stuffing

■ ■ ■

¼ pound bulk pork sausage
1¼ cups water
½ cup cooked whole kernel
  corn
½ cup shredded Cheddar
  cheese (2 ounces)
1 tablespoon chopped fresh
  parsley *or* 1 teaspoon
  dried parsley flakes
4 cups PEPPERIDGE FARM®
  Corn Bread Stuffing

1. In large saucepan over medium-high heat, cook sausage until browned, stirring to separate meat. Pour off fat.

2. Stir in water, corn, cheese and parsley. Add stuffing. Mix lightly. Spoon into greased 1½-quart casserole.

3. Cover and bake at 350°F. for 25 minutes or until hot.
Makes 6 servings

Tip: This stuffing bake brings a new flavor to the traditional holiday meal—and is easy enough for an everyday meal!

Prep Time: 15 minutes
Cook Time: 25 minutes

Country Corn Pudding

█ █ █

2 cups milk
¼ cup (½ stick) butter or
   margarine, melted
½ cup yellow cornmeal
1 tablespoon sugar
½ teaspoon salt
4 large eggs, beaten
2 tablespoons FRANK'S®
   REDHOT® Hot Sauce
1 can (11 ounces) Mexican-
   style corn, drained
1⅓ cups FRENCH'S® French
   Fried Onions, divided
1 cup (4 ounces) shredded
   Cheddar cheese
½ teaspoon baking powder
   Salsa (optional)

Whisk together milk, butter, cornmeal, sugar and salt in 3-quart microwave-safe bowl. Cover with vented plastic wrap and microwave on HIGH 8 minutes or until mixture is very thick and almost all of the liquid is absorbed, whisking twice. (Mixture should mound when dropped from a spoon.)

Combine eggs, Redhot® sauce, ⅔ cup French Fried Onions, cheese and baking powder in medium bowl. Stir egg mixture into cornmeal mixture; microwave, uncovered, on MEDIUM (50% power) 5 minutes or until knife inserted in center comes out clean. Sprinkle with remaining ⅔ cup onions. Microwave on MEDIUM 1 minute or until onions are golden. Serve with salsa, if desired.

Makes 6 side-dish sevings

Prep Time: 10 minutes
Cook Time: 20 minutes

Pine Nut Dressing

█ █ █

1 bag SUCCESS® White or
   Brown Rice
1 tablespoon reduced-calorie
   margarine
½ cup chopped onion
½ cup chopped celery
½ cup low sodium chicken
   broth
¼ cup pine nuts, toasted
1 tablespoon chopped fresh
   parsley
¾ teaspoon poultry seasoning
¼ teaspoon celery salt
¼ teaspoon pepper

Prepare rice according to package directions.

Melt margarine in large saucepan over medium heat. Add onion and celery; cook and stir until crisp-tender. Stir in rice and remaining ingredients. Reduce heat to low; simmer 10 minutes, stirring occasionally.

Makes 6 servings

Pepperidge Farm® Scalloped Apple Bake

▮▮▮

¼ **cup margarine** *or* **butter, melted**
¼ **cup sugar**
2 **teaspoons grated orange peel**
1 **teaspoon ground cinnamon**
1½ **cups PEPPERIDGE FARM® Corn Bread Stuffing**
½ **cup coarsely chopped pecans**
1 **can (16 ounces) whole berry cranberry sauce**
⅓ **cup orange juice** *or* **water**
4 **large cooking apples, cored and thinly sliced (about 6 cups)**

1. Lightly mix margarine, sugar, orange peel, cinnamon, stuffing and pecans and set aside.

2. Mix cranberry sauce, juice and apples. Add *half* the stuffing mixture. Mix lightly. Spoon into 8-inch square baking dish. Sprinkle remaining stuffing mixture over apple mixture.

3. Bake at 375°F. for 40 minutes or until apples are tender.

Makes 6 servings

Tip: To melt margarine, remove wrapper and place in microwave-safe cup. Cover and microwave on HIGH 45 seconds.

Prep Time: 25 minutes
Cook Time: 40 minutes

Cook's Notes

When grating orange peel, grate only the outer orange layer of the skin, which is very sweet and flavorful. Avoid grating into the white pith, as it is bitter tasting.

Top to bottom: Pepperidge Farm® Sausage Corn Bread Stuffing (page 20) and Pepperidge Farm® Scalloped Apple Bake

Green Beans with Blue Cheese and Roasted Peppers

▌▌▌

1 bag (20 ounces) frozen cut green beans
½ jar (about 3 ounces) roasted red pepper strips, drained and slivered
⅛ teaspoon salt
⅛ teaspoon white pepper
4 ounces cream cheese
½ cup milk
¾ cup blue cheese (3 ounces), crumbled
½ cup Italian-style bread crumbs
1 tablespoon butter or margarine, melted

Preheat oven to 350°F. Spray 2-quart oval casserole with nonstick cooking spray.

Combine green beans, red pepper strips, salt and pepper in prepared dish.

Place cream cheese and milk in small saucepan; cook and stir until cheese is melted. Add blue cheese; stir only until combined. Pour cheese mixture over green bean mixture and stir until green beans are coated.

Combine bread crumbs and butter in small bowl; sprinkle evenly over casserole.

Bake, uncovered, 20 minutes or until hot and bubbly.

Makes 4 servings

Serve It With Style!

 Give this dish a holiday look by garnishing it with diced red bell peppers and fresh parsley.

Green Beans with Blue Cheese and Roasted Peppers

Holiday Home Cooking

Cranberry Orange Game Hens with Vegetable Stuffing

▌▌▌

GAME HENS

4 small Cornish game hens
   (16 ounces each)
1 carrot, finely diced
1 stalk celery, finely diced
2 cups bread stuffing mix
1 teaspoon poultry seasoning
1 cup chicken stock or broth
  Salt and pepper

SAUCE

1 cup fresh or frozen
   cranberries, chopped
1 cup (12-ounce jar)
   SMUCKER'S® Sweet
   Orange Marmalade
¼ cup water
1 teaspoon lemon juice
  Lemon wedges (optional)

Remove as much fat as possible from game hens. Combine carrots, celery, stuffing mix, poultry seasoning and chicken stock. Season with salt and pepper. Fill cavity of each hen with stuffing; place on roasting pan. Bake at 400°F for 45 minutes.

Meanwhile, prepare sauce. In medium saucepan, combine all sauce ingredients. Cook over medium-high heat for 5 to 8 minutes until cranberries have released their juice. Set aside.

Remove game hens from oven. Spread sauce over top and sides of hens. Reserve any extra sauce to serve later with hens. Return hens to oven and continue baking 10 to 15 minutes.

To serve, place game hens on 4 serving plates. Spoon some of stuffing onto each plate. Spoon additional sauce over hens. Garnish with lemon wedges, if desired.

Makes 4 servings

Holiday Turkey with Herbed Corn Bread Dressing

█ █ █

1 pound bulk pork sausage
1½ cups chopped onions
1 cup chopped celery
6 cups coarsely crumbled
    corn bread (two 8-inch
    squares)
¼ cup dry sherry
⅓ cup light cream
1 teaspoon dried thyme
    leaves
1 teaspoon dried basil leaves
1 teaspoon dried oregano
    leaves
½ teaspoon LAWRY'S® Garlic
    Powder with Parsley
1 (14- to 16-pound) turkey,
    thawed
    LAWRY'S® Seasoned Salt

In large skillet, cook sausage until brown and crumbly; add onions and celery. Cook over medium heat 5 minutes or until tender. Add corn bread, sherry, cream, thyme, basil, oregano and Garlic Powder with Parsley. Rub cavities and outside of turkey with Seasoned Salt, using about ¼ teaspoon Seasoned Salt per pound of turkey. Pack dressing loosely into turkey cavity. Skewer opening closed. Insert meat thermometer in thickest part of breast away from bones. Place turkey, breast side up, on rack in roasting pan. Roast, uncovered, in 325°F oven 4 to 5 hours, basting frequently with melted butter, or cover with foil and place on hot grill 16 to 18 minutes per pound. When internal temperature reaches 185°F, remove and let stand 20 minutes before carving. (Tent loosely with aluminum foil if turkey becomes too brown, being careful not to touch meat thermometer.)

Makes 10 servings

Serving Suggestion: Garnish with lemon leaves and whole fresh cranberries.

Cook's Notes

It is always best to thaw a frozen turkey in the refrigerator. Estimate 24 hours of thawing time for every 5 pounds of bird.

Roast Leg of Lamb

▌▌▌

3 tablespoons coarse-grained
   mustard
2 cloves garlic, minced*
1½ teaspoons dried rosemary
   leaves, crushed
½ teaspoon freshly ground
   black pepper
1 leg of lamb, well trimmed,
   boned, rolled and tied
   (about 4 pounds)
Mint jelly (optional)

For more intense garlic flavor inside the meat, cut garlic into slivers. Cut small pockets at random intervals throughout roast with tip of sharp knife; insert garlic slivers.

Preheat oven to 400°F. Combine mustard, garlic, rosemary and pepper. Rub mustard mixture over lamb. Place roast on meat rack in shallow, foil-lined roasting pan. Insert meat thermometer in thickest part of roast. Roast 15 minutes. *Reduce oven temperature to 325°F;* roast 20 minutes per pound until thermometer registers 145°F for medium.

Transfer roast to carving board; tent with foil. Let stand 10 minutes before carving. Temperature will continue to rise 5° to 10°F during stand time.

Cut strings; discard. Carve roast into thin slices; serve with mint jelly, if desired.

Makes 6 to 8 servings

Cider-Glazed Cornish Hens

▌▌▌

6 PERDUE® Fresh Cornish
   Hens
Salt
Freshly ground pepper
1 quart apple cider or juice
1 cinnamon stick
2 tablespoons unsalted
   butter
2 tablespoons honey
1 tablespoon Dijon-style
   mustard
1 tablespoon red wine
   vinegar

Preheat oven to 375°F. Wash hens and pat dry with paper towel. Season inside and out with salt and pepper. Tie legs together and fold wings back. For glaze, place cider with cinnamon stick in medium saucepan; boil until reduced to 1 cup. Remove cinnamon stick and stir in butter, honey, mustard and vinegar. Boil until thick, syrupy and translucent.

Place hens in shallow roasting pan. Roast hens, brushing occasionally with glaze, 55 to 60 minutes or until golden and tender. *Makes 6 servings*

Apple & Onion-Stuffed Chicken

▊▊▊

1 whole chicken
    (3¾ pounds)
½ teaspoon salt
½ teaspoon ground black
    pepper
1 large Granny Smith apple,
    peeled, cored and thinly
    sliced
1 large onion, sliced
1 package (5 ounces)
    poultry blend
¼ cup fresh lemon juice
2 tablespoons unsalted
    butter

1. Preheat oven to 425°F. Spray large roasting pan and rack with nonstick cooking spray. Rinse the chicken and pat dry with paper towels. Season body and neck cavities salt and pepper. Combine apple and onion in small bowl.

2. Gently loosen skin from breast and stuff half of the apple-onion mixture under the skin.

3. Stuff the remaining apple-onion mixture into body and neck cavities. Place poultry blend in the body cavity. Fold wings over brest and tie legs together. Place chicken on rack, breast side up, in roasting pan. In a small saucepan, whisk the lemon juice and butter over medium heat until melted. Brush on the chicken. Roast for 45 minutes or until golden brown.

4. Reduce the oven temperature to 350°F and continue to roast, basting frequently with the pan drippings, for 1 hour or until meat thermometer inserted into thickest part of thigh, not touching any bone registers 180°F. Let the chicken stand 10 to 15 minutes. Remove apple-onion stuffing from cavity; discard poultry blend.

5. Carve chicken, Serve with apple-onion stuffing.

Makes 8 servings

Apple & Onion-Stuffed Chicken

Herb-Roasted Racks of Lamb

███

½ cup mango chutney, chopped

2 to 3 cloves garlic, minced

2 whole racks (6 ribs each) lamb loin chops (2½ to 3 pounds)

1 cup fresh French or Italian bread crumbs

1 tablespoon chopped fresh thyme *or* 1 teaspoon dried thyme leaves

1 tablespoon chopped fresh rosemary *or* 1 teaspoon dried rosemary

1 tablespoon chopped fresh oregano *or* 1 teaspoon dried oregano

1. Preheat oven to 400°F. Combine chutney and garlic in small bowl; spread evenly over meaty side of lamb with thin spatula. Combine remaining ingredients in separate small bowl; pat crumb mixture evenly over chutney mixture.

2. Place lamb racks, crumb sides up, on rack in shallow roasting pan. Roast in oven about 30 minutes or until instant-read thermometer inserted into lamb, but not touching bone, registers 145°F for medium or to desired doneness.

3. Place lamb on carving board; tent with foil. Let racks stand about 10 minutes for easier slicing. Internal temperature will continue to rise about 5° to 10°F during stand time. Slice between ribs into individual chops with large carving knife. Garnish with additional fresh herbs and mango slices, if desired. Serve immediately.

Makes 4 servings

Serve It With Style!

*R*ub lamb bones with olive oil prior to roasting. When you remove the roast from the oven, the bones will have a nice shine and be deep brown in color.

Roast Turkey with Sweet Vegetable Purée

▌▌▌

¼ cup parve margarine
1 large onion, coarsely chopped
4 ribs celery, sliced
1 Granny Smith apple, coarsely chopped
1 package (11 ounces) dried fruit mix, chopped
1 cup slivered almonds or chopped walnuts
⅓ cup chopped fresh parsley
¼ teaspoon ground cloves
Salt
Freshly ground black pepper
1 whole turkey (12 to 14 pounds)
6 medium sweet potatoes, peeled, cut into 1-inch pieces
6 to 8 carrots, thickly sliced
5 large shallots, peeled
½ cup kosher dry white wine (optional)

Preheat oven to 325°F. Melt margarine in large saucepan over medium heat. Add onion; cook, stirring occasionally, 8 minutes or until tender. Remove from heat; stir in celery, apple, fruit mix, almonds, parsley and cloves. Add salt and pepper to taste.

Place fruit mixture in turkey cavity. Tie turkey legs together with kitchen string. Place turkey, breast side down, on rack in large oiled roasting pan. Season with salt and pepper, if desired. Add ½ cup water to pan. Bake, uncovered, 1½ hours.

Remove turkey from roasting pan; remove rack. Return turkey; breast side up, to roasting pan. Arrange sweet potatoes, carrots and shallots around turkey; season with salt and pepper, if desired. Baste turkey with pan juices. Add wine to roasting pan, if desired. Bake 2 to 2½ hours or until internal temperature of thigh meat reaches 180°F and legs move easily, basting with pan juices every 30 minutes.

Remove turkey to cutting board; tent with foil. Let stand 10 minutes. Remove vegetables from pan with slotted spoon to food processor; process until smooth. Remove fruit stuffing from turkey cavity. Slice turkey. Serve with vegetable purée and fruit stuffing.

Makes 12 servings

Favorite recipe from **Hebrew National**®

Roast Turkey with Sweet Vegetable Purée

Prime Rib with Horseradish Cream Sauce

■ ■ ■

Horseradish Cream Sauce
(recipe follows)
3 cloves garlic, minced
1 teaspoon ground black
    pepper
3 rib standing beef roast,
    trimmed* (about 6 to
    7 pounds)

Prepare Horseradish Cream Sauce. Preheat oven to 450°F. Combine garlic and pepper; rub over surfaces of roast.

Place roast bone side down in shallow roasting pan. Insert meat thermometer in thickest part of roast, not touching bone or fat. Roast 15 minutes.

Reduce oven temperature to 325°F. Roast 20 minutes per pound or until internal temperature is 145°F for medium.

When roast has reached desired temperature, transfer to cutting board; tent with foil. Let stand in warm place 15 to 20 minutes to allow for easier carving. Temperature of roast will continue to rise about 10°F during stand time. Serve with Horseradish Cream Sauce.

Makes 6 to 8 servings

HORSERADISH CREAM SAUCE

1 cup whipping cream
⅓ cup prepared horseradish,
    undrained
2 teaspoons balsamic or red
    wine vinegar
1 teaspoon dry mustard
¼ teaspoon sugar
⅛ teaspoon salt

Beat cream until soft peaks form. *Do not overbeat.* Combine horseradish, vinegar, mustard, sugar and salt in medium bowl. Fold whipped cream into horseradish mixture. Cover and refrigerate at least 1 hour. Sauce may be made up to 8 hours before serving.   *Makes 1½ cups*

Cook's Notes

For extra flavor, rub fresh herbs, such as chopped thyme leaves and rosemary, onto the meat prior to roasting.

Pork Roast with Corn Bread & Oyster Stuffing

■ ■ ■

1 (5- to 7-pound) pork loin roast*
2 tablespoons butter *or* margarine
½ cup chopped onion
½ cup chopped celery
2 cloves garlic, minced
½ teaspoon fennel seeds, crushed
1 teaspoon TABASCO® brand Pepper Sauce
½ teaspoon salt
2 cups packaged corn bread stuffing mix
1 (8-ounce) can oysters, undrained, chopped

Have butcher crack backbone of pork loin roast.

Preheat oven to 325°F. Make a deep slit in back of each chop on pork loin. Melt butter in large saucepan; add onion, celery, garlic and fennel seeds. Cook 5 minutes or until vegetables are tender; stir in TABASCO® Sauce and salt. Add stuffing mix, oysters and oyster liquid; toss to mix well.

Stuff corn bread mixture into slits in pork. (Any leftover stuffing may be baked in covered baking dish during last 30 minutes of roasting.)

Place meat in shallow roasting pan. Cook 30 to 35 minutes per pound or until instant-read thermometer inserted into pork roast registers 170°F. Remove to serving platter. Allow meat to stand 15 minutes before carving.

Makes 12 servings

Serve It With Style!

The Cranberry-Apple Chutney recipe (on page 10) would make a scrumptious addition to this delicious holiday roast.

Holidays Around the World

Spanish Churros

▮▮▮

1 cup water
¼ cup butter or margarine
6 tablespoons sugar, divided
¼ teaspoon salt
1 cup all-purpose flour
2 large eggs
   Vegetable oil for frying
1 teaspoon ground cinnamon

Place water, butter, 2 tablespoons sugar and salt in medium saucepan; bring to a boil over high heat. Remove from heat; add flour. Beat with spoon until dough forms ball and releases from side of pan. Vigorously beat in eggs, 1 at a time, until mixture is smooth. Spoon dough into pastry bag fitted with large star tip. Pipe 3×1-inch strips onto waxed-paper-lined baking sheet. Place baking sheet in freezer; freeze 20 minutes.

Pour vegetable oil into 10-inch skillet to ¾-inch depth. Heat oil to 375°F. Transfer frozen dough to hot oil with large spatula. Fry 4 or 5 cookies at a time until deep golden brown, 3 to 4 minutes, turning once. Remove cookies with spatula to paper towels; drain.

Combine remaining 4 tablespoons sugar with cinnamon. Place in paper bag. Add warm cookies 1 at a time; close bag and shake until cookie is coated with sugar mixture. Repeat with remaining sugar mixture and cookies. Remove cookies to wire racks; cool completely. Store tightly covered at room temperature or freeze up to 3 months.
   Makes about 3 dozen cookies

Linzer Torte

▌▌▌

1 cup slivered almonds
**1¼ cups unsifted all-purpose
flour**
¼ cup sugar
2 eggs
½ cup butter, softened
**1 tablespoon grated lemon
peel**
½ teaspoon almond extract
**¾ cup SMUCKER'S® Apricot
Preserves**
**¼ cup SMUCKER'S® Red
Raspberry Preserves**

Finely chop almonds in food
processor or blender. Lightly
spoon flour into measuring
cup; level off. In food
processor or large bowl of
electric mixer, stir together
almonds, flour and sugar.

Separate one egg; set white
aside. Add egg yolk, remaining
whole egg, butter, lemon peel
and almond extract to flour
mixture. Process or mix until
dough forms a ball.

Remove scant ⅓ of dough;
flatten, wrap and refrigerate
for at least ½ hour or until
manageable.

Grease 9-inch round tart pan
with removable bottom. Press
remaining dough in bottom
and about ½ inch up sides of
pan. Spread ½ cup of the
apricot preserves evenly over
dough.

Remove refrigerated dough.
On floured surface or between
sheets of waxed paper, roll into
9½×5-inch rectangle. Cut into
ten (½-inch-wide) strips. Place
one strip across center of torte.
Place second strip on each
side, about 2 inches in from
edge. Repeat in other
direction. Now place a strip
between center and edge strips
in each direction. Press strips
to edge. Trim off evenly with
knife or pastry wheel.

Brush strips with reserved egg
white. Spoon remaining
apricot preserves and
raspberry preserves in
alternate spaces between
strips.

Bake at 350° for 30 minutes or
until crust is golden brown.
Cool 10 minutes. Remove sides
of pan. Serve warm or cool.
Keeps for up to 1 week, tightly
covered.

Makes 10 servings

Note: If crust bubbles up
during baking, poke with
wooden pick to break bubbles.

Oysters Romano

12 oysters, shucked and on
   the half shell
   Salt
2 slices bacon, cut into
   12 (1-inch) pieces
½ cup Italian-seasoned dry
   bread crumbs
2 tablespoons butter or
   margarine, melted
½ teaspoon garlic salt
6 tablespoons grated
   Romano, Parmesan or
   provolone cheese
Fresh chives for garnish

Preheat oven to 375°F. Place shells with oysters on baking sheet. Top each oyster with 1 piece bacon. Bake 10 minutes or until bacon is crisp. Meanwhile, combine bread crumbs, butter and garlic salt in small bowl. Spoon mixture over oysters; top with cheese. Bake 5 to 10 minutes or until cheese melts. Serve immediately. Garnish with chives, if desired.

Makes 4 appetizer servings

ters Romano

Classic Brisket Tzimmes

▌▌▌

2 first cut (about 2½ pounds each) or 1 whole HEBREW NATIONAL® Fresh Brisket (about 5 to 6 pounds), well trimmed
1 teaspoon salt
½ teaspoon freshly ground black pepper
2 tablespoons vegetable oil
1 large onion, chopped
3 cloves garlic, minced
2 cups beef or chicken broth
½ cup orange juice
2 tablespoons light brown sugar
2 tablespoons fresh lemon juice
1 tablespoon tomato paste
1 teaspoon dried thyme leaves
1 teaspoon ground cinnamon
¼ teaspoon ground cloves
6 to 8 medium carrots, peeled, sliced
3 medium sweet potatoes, peeled, cut into ½-inch-thick slices
8 ounces dried pitted prunes

Preheat oven to 325°F. Place brisket in large roasting pan; sprinkle with salt and pepper. Heat oil in medium saucepan over medium-high heat. Add onion and garlic; cook and stir 8 minutes. Stir in broth, orange juice, brown sugar, lemon juice, tomato paste, thyme, cinnamon and cloves. Bring to a boil, stirring occasionally. Pour evenly over brisket. Cover; bake 1½ hours.

Add carrots, sweet potatoes and prunes to pan. Cover; bake 1 to 1½ hours or until brisket and vegetables are fork-tender. Transfer brisket to cutting board; tent with foil. Spoon pan juices over fruit and vegetables; transfer to serving platter. Skim fat from pan juices; discard fat.

Slice brisket across the grain into ¼-inch-thick slices; transfer to serving platter. Spoon sauce over brisket and vegetables.

Makes 10 to 12 servings

Classic Brisket Tzimmes

Dutch St. Nicolas Cookies

▌▌▌

½ cup whole natural almonds
¾ cup butter or margarine, softened
½ cup packed brown sugar
2 tablespoons milk
1½ teaspoons ground cinnamon
¼ teaspoon ground nutmeg
¼ teaspoon ground ginger
¼ teaspoon ground cloves
2 cups sifted all-purpose flour
1½ teaspoons baking powder
½ teaspoon salt
¼ cup coarsely chopped citron

Spread almonds in single layer on baking sheet. Bake at 375°F, 10 to 12 minutes, stirring occasionally, until lightly toasted. Cool. Chop finely. In large bowl, cream butter, sugar, milk and spices. In small bowl, combine flour, baking powder and salt. Add flour mixture to creamed mixture; blend well. Stir in almonds and citron. Knead dough slightly to make ball. Cover; refrigerate until firm. Roll out dough ¼ inch thick on lightly floured surface. Cut out with cookie cutters. Place 2 inches apart on greased cookie sheets. Bake at 375°F, 7 to 10 minutes, until lightly browned. Remove to wire racks; cool.
Makes about 3½ dozen cookies

Favorite recipe from **Almond Board of California**

Mexican Shrimp Cocktail

▌▌▌

½ cup WISH-BONE® Italian Dressing*
½ cup chopped tomato
1 can (4 ounces) chopped green chilies, undrained
¼ cup chopped green onions
1½ teaspoons honey
¼ teaspoon hot pepper sauce
1 pound medium shrimp, shelled and deveined, cooked
2 teaspoons finely chopped coriander (cilantro) or parsley

*Also terrific with WISH-BONE® Robusto Italian or Lite Italian Dressing.

In medium bowl, combine Italian dressing, tomato, chilies with liquid, green onions, honey and hot pepper sauce. Stir in shrimp. Cover and marinate in refrigerator, stirring occasionally, at least 2 hours. Just before serving, stir in coriander.
Makes about 6 servings

Hanukkah Fried Cruller Bows

INGREDIENTS
1¼ cups all-purpose flour
3 tablespoons powdered sugar
2 tablespoons granulated sugar
½ teaspoon salt
1 egg
2 egg whites
1 teaspoon vanilla
Vegetable oil, for frying
Powdered sugar
Ground cinnamon

SUPPLIES
Deep-frying thermometer

1. Combine flour, 3 tablespoons powdered sugar, granulated sugar and salt in small bowl. Stir in egg, egg whites and vanilla with fork until mixture is crumbly.

2. Form dough into ball; knead on lightly floured surface until smooth, about 5 minutes. Cover loosely; let stand about 30 minutes.

3. Heat 2 inches oil to 375°F in heavy, large saucepan. Roll dough on floured surface to 12×12-inch square, about ⅛-inch thick. Cut into 12 (1-inch) strips; cut strips in half to form 24 (6×1-inch) strips. Tie strips into knots.

4. Fry knots in oil, a few at a time, 3 to 4 minutes or until golden. Drain on paper towels. Sprinkle with powdered sugar and cinnamon. Serve warm.
Makes 2 dozen bows

Cook's Nook

For a sweet variation, sprinkle ground cinnamon or nutmeg or a combination of powdered sugar, nutmeg and ground cinnamon on some bows.

COOKIE COLLECTION

Star Christmas Tree Cookies

COOKIES
   ½ cup vegetable shortening
   ⅓ cup butter or margarine, softened
   2 egg yolks
   1 teaspoon vanilla extract
   1 package DUNCAN HINES® Moist Deluxe Yellow or Devil's Food Cake Mix
   1 tablespoon water

FROSTING
   1 container (16 ounces) DUNCAN HINES® Creamy Homestyle Vanilla Frosting
   Green food coloring
   Red and green sugar crystals for garnish
   Assorted colored candies and decors for garnish

Preheat oven to 375°F. For Cookies, combine shortening, butter, egg yolks and vanilla extract. Blend in cake mix gradually. Add 1 teaspoonful water at a time until dough is rolling consistency. Divide dough into 4 balls. Flatten one ball with hand; roll to ⅛-inch thickness on lightly floured surface. Cut with graduated star cookie cutters. Repeat using remaining dough. Bake large cookies together on *ungreased* baking sheet. Bake 6 to 8 minutes or until edges are light golden brown. Cool cookies 1 minute. Remove from baking sheet. Repeat with smaller cookies, testing for doneness at minimum baking time.

For Frosting, tint vanilla frosting with green food coloring. Frost cookies and stack, beginning with largest cookies on bottom and ending with smallest cookies on top. Rotate cookies when stacking to alternate corners. Decorate as desired with colored sugar crystals and assorted colored candies and decors.
   Makes 2 to 3 dozen cookies

Chocolate-Nut Squares

███

1 cup (6 ounces) semisweet
    chocolate chips
1 cup milk chocolate chips
1 tablespoon shortening
1 package (14 ounces)
    caramels
2 tablespoons butter or
    margarine
3 tablespoons milk
2 cups coarsely chopped
    pecans

Line 8-inch square pan with buttered foil; set aside. Melt both kinds of chips with shortening in heavy, small saucepan over very low heat, stirring constantly. Spoon half the chocolate mixture into prepared pan, spreading evenly over bottom and ¼ inch up sides of pan. Refrigerate until firm.

Meanwhile, combine caramels, butter and milk in heavy, medium saucepan. Cook over medium heat, stirring constantly. When mixture is smooth, stir in pecans. Cool to lukewarm. Spread caramel mixture evenly over chocolate in pan. Melt remaining chocolate mixture again over very low heat, stirring constantly; spread over caramel layer. Refrigerate until almost firm. Cut into squares. Store in refrigerator.

Makes about 2 pounds

Cook's Notes

Squares are less likely to break apart if the chocolate is not completely firm when you cut them. Rinse the knife under hot water and wipe it clean after each cut.

Chocolate Peppermints (page 74)
and Chocolate Nut Squares

Peppermint Puffs

▮▮▮

1 cup firmly packed light brown sugar
¾ Butter Flavor* CRISCO® Stick or ¾ cup Butter Flavor* CRISCO® all-vegetable shortening
2 tablespoons milk
1 tablespoon vanilla
1 egg
1¾ cups all-purpose flour
1 teaspoon salt
¾ teaspoon baking soda
⅔ cup crushed peppermint candy canes**

* Butter Flavor Crisco is artificially flavored.

** To crush candy canes, break into small pieces. Place in plastic food storage bag. Secure top. Use rolling pin to break candy into very small pieces.

1. Heat oven to 375°F. Place sheets of foil on counter top for cooling cookies.

2. Combine brown sugar, ¾ cup shortening, milk and vanilla in large bowl. Beat at medium speed of electric mixer until well blended. Beat egg into creamed mixture.

3. Combine flour, salt and baking soda. Mix into creamed mixture at low speed just until blended. Stir in crushed candy.

4. Shape dough into 1-inch balls. Place 2 inches apart on ungreased baking sheet.

5. Bake one baking sheet at a time at 375°F for 8 to 10 minutes for chewy cookies or 11 to 13 minutes for crisp cookies. *Do not overbake.* Cool 2 minutes on baking sheet. Remove cookies to foil to cool completely.
   Makes about 3 dozen cookies

Holiday Pineapple Cheese Bars

▌▌▌

¼ cup butter or margarine
¼ cup packed brown sugar
¾ cup flour
¾ cup finely chopped
    macadamia nuts
1 (8-ounce) can crushed
    pineapple, undrained
1 (8-ounce) package
    PHILADELPHIA® Cream
    Cheese, softened
¼ cup granulated sugar
1 egg
1 cup BAKER'S® ANGEL
    FLAKE® Coconut
½ cup coarsely chopped
    macadamia nuts
1 tablespoon butter or
    margarine, melted

• Preheat oven to 350°F.

• Beat ¼ cup butter and brown sugar in small mixing bowl at medium speed with electric mixer until well blended. Add flour and ¾ cup finely chopped nuts; mix well. Press onto bottom of 9-inch square baking pan. Bake 10 minutes. Cool.

• Drain pineapple, reserving 2 tablespoons liquid.

• Beat cream cheese, reserved liquid, granulated sugar and egg in small mixing bowl at medium speed with electric mixer until well blended. Stir in pineapple. Pour over crust.

• Sprinkle with combined coconut, ½ cup coarsely chopped nuts and 1 tablespoon butter.

• Bake 18 minutes. Cool completely. Cut into bars.
    Makes about 1½ dozen bars

Prep Time: 20 minutes
Cook Time: 18 minutes

Chocolate Spritz Cookies

▌▌▌

1 package DUNCAN HINES®
   Golden Sugar Cookie Mix
⅓ cup unsweetened cocoa
1 egg
⅓ cup vegetable oil
2 tablespoons water

1. Preheat oven to 375°F.

2. Combine cookie mix and cocoa in large mixing bowl. Stir until blended. Add egg, oil and water. Stir until thoroughly blended.

3. Fill cookie press with dough. Press desired shapes 2 inches apart onto ungreased cookie sheets. Bake at 375°F for 6 to 8 minutes or until set. Cool 1 minute on baking sheets. Remove to cooling racks. Cool completely.

Makes 5 to 6 dozen cookies

NOTE: For a delicious no-cholesterol variation, substitute 2 egg whites for whole egg.

TIP: For festive cookies, decorate before baking with assorted decors or after baking with melted milk chocolate or semi-sweet chocolate, or white chocolate and chopped nuts.

Chocolate-Pecan Angels

▌▌▌

1 cup mini semisweet
   chocolate chips
1 cup chopped pecans,
   toasted
1 cup sifted powdered sugar
1 egg white

Preheat oven to 350°F. Grease cookie sheets. Combine chips, pecans and powdered sugar in medium bowl. Add egg white; mix well. Drop batter by teaspoonfuls 2 inches apart onto prepared cookie sheets.

Bake 11 to 12 minutes until edges are light golden brown. Let cookies stand on cookie sheets 1 minute. Remove cookies to wire racks; cool completely.

Makes about 3 dozen cookies

Chocolate Spritz Cookies

Gingerbread Kids

▌▌▌

2 ripe, small DOLE® Bananas
4 cups all-purpose flour
1½ teaspoons ground ginger
1 teaspoon baking soda
1 teaspoon ground cinnamon
½ cup butter, softened
½ cup packed brown sugar
½ cup dark molasses
Prepared icing and candies

• Purée bananas in blender. Combine flour, ginger, baking soda and cinnamon. Cream butter and sugar until light and fluffy. Beat in molasses and bananas until blended. Stir in flour mixture with wooden spoon until completely blended. (Dough will be stiff.) Cover; refrigerate 1 hour.

• Preheat oven to 375°F. Divide dough into 4 parts. Roll out each part to ⅛-inch thickness on lightly floured surface. Cut out cookies using small gingerbread people cutters. Use favorite cookie cutters for any smaller amounts of remaining dough.

• Bake on greased cookie sheets 10 to 15 minutes or until just brown around edges. Cool completely on wire racks. Decorate as desired with favorite icing and candies.
Makes 30 to 35 cookies

Cook's Nook

These classic holiday cookies would make fun Christmas tree ornaments. To make cookie ornaments, remove baked cookies from the oven, then gently place a drinking straw through the top section of each cookie. Once all the cookies have a hole in them, remove them from the cookie sheet to wire racks. Cool completely before frosting.

Christmas Ornament Cookies

■ ■ ■

2¼ cups all-purpose flour
¼ teaspoon salt
1 cup sugar
¾ cup butter, softened
1 large egg
1 teaspoon vanilla
1 teaspoon almond extract
Icing (recipe follows)
Assorted candies or decors

Place flour and salt in medium bowl; stir to combine. Beat sugar and butter in large bowl with electric mixer at medium speed until light and fluffy. Beat in egg, vanilla and almond extract. Gradually add flour mixture. Beat at low speed until well blended. Divide dough in half; cover and refrigerate 30 minutes or until firm.

Preheat oven to 350°F. Working with 1 portion at a time, roll out dough on lightly floured surface to ¼-inch thickness. Cut dough into desired shapes with assorted floured cookie cutters. Reroll trimmings and cut out more cookies. Place cutouts on ungreased baking sheets. Using drinking straw or tip of sharp knife, cut hole near top of each cookie to allow for piece of ribbon or string to be inserted for hanger. Bake 10 to 12 minutes or until edges are golden brown. Let cookies stand on baking sheets 1 minute. Remove cookies to wire racks; cool completely.

Prepare Icing. Spoon Icing into small resealable plastic food storage bag. Cut off very tiny corner of bag; pipe Icing decoratively over cookies. Decorate with candies as desired. Let stand at room temperature 40 minutes or until set. Thread ribbon through each cookie hole to hang as Christmas tree ornaments.
Makes about 2 dozen cookies

ICING
2 cups powdered sugar
2 tablespoons milk or lemon juice
Food coloring (optional)

Place powdered sugar and milk in small bowl; stir with spoon until smooth. (Icing will be very thick. If it is too thick, stir in 1 teaspoon additional milk.) Divide into small bowls and tint with food coloring, if desired.

Chocolate Chip Walnut Bars

▌▌▌

Bar Cookie Crust (recipe
   follows)
2 eggs
½ cup KARO® Light or Dark
   Corn Syrup
½ cup sugar
2 tablespoons MAZOLA®
   Margarine or butter,
   melted
1 cup (6 ounces) semisweet
   chocolate chips
¾ cup chopped walnuts

1. Preheat oven to 350°F.
Prepare Bar Cookie Crust.

2. Meanwhile, in medium bowl
beat eggs, corn syrup, sugar
and margarine until well
blended. Stir in chocolate
chips and walnuts. Pour over
hot crust; spread evenly.

3. Bake 15 to 18 minutes or
until set. Cool completely on
wire rack. Cut into 2×1½-inch
bars.   *Makes about 32 bars*

Prep Time: 30 minutes
Bake Time: 30 minutes, plus
cooling

BAR COOKIE CRUST

MAZOLA NO STICK®
   Cooking Spray
2 cups flour
½ cup (1 stick) cold
   MAZOLA® Margarine or
   butter, cut into pieces
⅓ cup sugar
¼ teaspoon salt

1. Preheat oven to 350°F. Spray
13×9-inch baking pan with
cooking spray.

2. In large bowl with mixer at
medium speed, beat flour,
margarine, sugar and salt until
mixture resembles coarse
crumbs. Press firmly into
bottom and ¼ inch up sides of
prepared pan.

3. Bake 15 minutes or until
golden brown. Top with
desired filling. Complete as
recipe directs.

Prep Time: 10 minutes
Bake Time: 15 minutes

Holiday Fruit Drops

▌▌▌

½ cup butter, softened
¾ cup packed brown sugar
1 egg
1¼ cups all-purpose flour
1 teaspoon vanilla
½ teaspoon baking soda
½ teaspoon ground cinnamon
  Pinch salt
1 cup (8 ounces) diced
  candied pineapple
1 cup (8 ounces) whole red
  and green candied
  cherries
8 ounces chopped pitted
  dates
1 cup (6 ounces) semisweet
  chocolate chips
½ cup whole hazelnuts
½ cup pecan halves
½ cup coarsely chopped
  walnuts

Preheat oven to 325°F. Lightly grease cookie sheets or line with parchment paper. Cream butter and sugar in large bowl. Beat in egg until light and fluffy. Mix in flour, vanilla, baking soda, cinnamon and salt. Stir in pineapple, cherries, dates, chocolate chips, hazelnuts, pecans and walnuts. Drop dough by rounded teaspoonfuls 2 inches apart onto prepared cookie sheets.

Bake 15 to 20 minutes or until firm and lightly browned around edges. Remove to wire racks to cool completely.

Makes about 8 dozen cookies

Cook's Nook

Home-baked cookies make great inexpensive gifts for friends and family. You can layer them on red or green tissue and present them in a decorative tin or gift box.

KITCHEN TOOL TIME   STAND MIXER

Kitchen tools come and go. Some work and some don't—most end up collecting dust because they are hard to use and tough to clean.

One tool that has stood the test of time is the stand mixer. You may have watched your grandmother use one as she was mixing dough for your favorite holiday bread. Mom probably let you scrape the bowl clean after she whipped up one of her special cake frostings. You may have received one as a wedding gift and never used it. Whatever the situation, the stand mixer is definitely a kitchen tool worth examining.

Thanks to American ingenuity, we have several choices when it comes to stand mixers. Before purchasing one, do your homework. Decide how often you bake and the type baking you do. Less expensive mixers may be the right choice for casual bakers, while the more expensive models with a variety of attachments may suit more serious bakers.

Why a stand mixer over a portable one?

Stand mixers offer several advantages over portable mixers. First, all stand mixers offer hands-free operation, allowing you to work on other parts of the recipe while batters and dough are mixing. Second, the design provides for more even mixing, and finally, since the machine is stationary, the chance for accidental spills is also reduced.

Which attachments do I need?

This choice depends on both the model you choose and the types of baking you do. Less expensive models may only come with beaters. For the occasional baker this is really the only attachment you will need. You can easily make most cake and cookie batters, frostings and icings with the beater attachment.

Bread bakers and serious cake makers might want to purchase a model with interchangeable attachments. The three most common are the whisk, paddle and dough hook; each is designed for a specific mixing technique.

The *whisk* incorporates air into liquid mixtures, such as egg whites and cream. As the whisk rotates faster the mixture becomes thicker and creamier. Meringues, frostings and thick sauces are all made using this attachment.

The *paddle* is used for mixing thicker and heavier cookie and cake batters where the incorporation of air is not critical to the recipe.

The *dough hook* is used mixing bread dough of all kinds. The design of the hook is excellent for pulling sticky dough away from the side of the mixing bowl.

All models come with a large mixing bowl; some come with extra smaller mixing bowls.

How many speeds do I need?

A simple way to determine the number of speeds you might require is to think of speed in ranges of slow, medium and fast. A model with numerous speeds is really just offering more speeds in each range.

What else should I know about stand mixers?

Whether you purchase an inexpensive model or a deluxe one with all the attachments, remember that the mixer is only a tool. Always follow the recipe. Most recipes call for exact ingredient amounts, so measure carefully.

If the model you purchase does not have a timer, it's probably a good idea to purchase one. The timer will help ensure that you are beating the mixture to the correct consistency.

It is always a good idea to clean as you go; batters dry quickly and make cleanup more difficult.

Your baking magic can begin, now that you're better acquainted with this helpful and easy-to-use kitchen tool.

COOKING CLASS

Caramel-Cinnamon Snack Mix

▌▌▌

2 tablespoons vegetable oil
½ cup popcorn kernels
½ teaspoon salt, divided
1½ cups packed light brown sugar
½ cup butter or margarine
½ cup corn syrup
¼ cup red hot cinnamon candies
2 cups cinnamon-flavored shaped graham crackers
1 cup red and green candy-coated chocolate pieces

Stir and melt candies with spoon.

Spread popcorn in even layer.

1. Grease 2 large baking pans; set aside.

2. Heat oil in large saucepan over high heat until hot. Add corn kernels. Cover pan. Shake pan constantly over heat until kernels no longer pop. Divide popcorn evenly between 2 large bowls. Add ¼ teaspoon salt to each bowl; toss to coat. Set aside.

3. Preheat oven to 250°F. Combine sugar, butter and corn syrup in heavy, medium saucepan. Cook over medium heat until sugar melts, stirring constantly with wooden spoon. Bring mixture to a boil. Boil 5 minutes, stirring frequently.

4. Remove ½ of sugar mixture (about ¾ cup) from saucepan; pour over 1 portion of popcorn. Toss with lightly greased spatula until evenly coated.

5. Add red hot candies to saucepan. Stir constantly with wooden spoon until melted. Pour over remaining portion of popcorn; toss with lightly greased spatula until evenly coated.

6. Spread each portion of popcorn in even layer in separate prepared pans with lightly greased spatula.

7. Bake 1 hour, stirring every 15 minutes with wooden spoon to prevent popcorn from sticking together. Cool completely in pans. Combine popcorn, graham crackers and chocolate pieces in large bowl. Store in airtight container at room temperature up to 1 week. *Makes about 4 quarts*

Serve It With Style!

Serve this snack mix at holiday gatherings or give it as delicious gift as shown in the photo. The decorative metal tin might be the perfect present for your letter carrier or as an office grab bag gift. The smaller cellophane wrapped portions would fit nicely into the kids' stockings or make festive party favors. Craft stores should carry all the supplies you'll need to turn these tasty treats into heartwarming holiday gifts.

Candy Cane LANE

Holiday Peppermint Candies

■ ■ ■

4 ounces PHILADELPHIA® Cream Cheese, softened
1 tablespoon butter or margarine
1 tablespoon light corn syrup
¼ teaspoon peppermint extract *or* few drops
    peppermint oil
4 cups powdered sugar
  Green and red food coloring
  Sifted powdered sugar
  Green, red and white decorating icing (optional)

MIX cream cheese, butter, corn syrup and extract in large mixing bowl with electric mixer on medium speed until well blended. Gradually add 4 cups powdered sugar; mix well.

DIVIDE mixture into thirds. Knead a few drops green food coloring into first third; repeat with red food coloring and second third. Wrap each third in plastic wrap.

SHAPE into I-inch balls, working with 1 color mixture at a time. Place on wax paper-lined cookie sheet. Flatten each ball with bottom of glass that has been lightly dipped in sifted powdered sugar.

REPEAT with remaining mixtures. Decorate with icing. Store candies in refrigerator.

Makes 5 dozen candies

Prep Time: 30 minutes plus refrigerating

Mint Truffles

1 package (10 ounces) mint chocolate chips
⅓ cup whipping cream
¼ cup butter or margarine
1 container (3½ ounces) chocolate sprinkles

Line baking sheet with waxed paper; set aside. Melt chips with whipping cream and butter in heavy, medium saucepan over low heat, stirring occasionally. Pour into pie pan. Refrigerate until mixture is fudgy, but soft, about 2 hours.

Shape about 1 tablespoonful mixture into 1¼-inch ball. To shape, roll mixture between palms. Repeat procedure with remaining mixture. Place balls on waxed paper.

Place sprinkles in shallow bowl; roll balls in sprinkles. Place truffles in petit four or candy cups. (If sprinkles won't stick because truffle has set, roll truffle between palms until outside is soft.) Truffles may be refrigerated 2 to 3 days or frozen several weeks.

Makes about 24 truffles

Almond Butter Crunch

1 cup BLUE DIAMOND® Blanched Slivered Almonds
½ cup butter
½ cup sugar
1 tablespoon light corn syrup

Line bottom and sides of 8- or 9-inch cake pan with aluminum foil (not plastic wrap or wax paper). Butter foil heavily; set aside. Combine almonds, butter, sugar and corn syrup in 10-inch skillet. Bring to a boil over medium heat, stirring constantly. Boil, stirring constantly, until mixture turns golden brown, about 5 to 6 minutes. Working quickly, spread candy in prepared pan. Cool about 15 minutes or until firm. Remove candy from pan by lifting edges of foil. Peel off foil. Cool thoroughly. Break into pieces.

Makes about ¾ pound

Butterscotch-Chocolate Divinity

▌▌▌

2 cups sugar
⅓ cup light corn syrup
⅓ cup water
2 egg whites
⅛ teaspoon cream of tartar
1 teaspoon vanilla
½ cup milk chocolate chips
½ cup butterscotch chips
½ cup chopped nuts

Line 2 or 3 baking sheets with buttered waxed paper; set aside. Combine sugar, corn syrup and water in heavy, medium saucepan. Cook over medium heat, stirring constantly, until sugar dissolves and mixture comes to a boil. Wash down side of pan frequently with pastry brush dipped in hot water to remove sugar crystals. Add candy thermometer. Continue to cook until mixture reaches the hard-ball stage (255°F).

Meanwhile, beat egg whites and cream of tartar with heavy-duty electric mixer until stiff but not dry. Slowly pour hot syrup into egg whites, beating constantly. Add vanilla; beat until candy forms soft peaks and starts to lose its gloss. Stir in both kinds of chips and nuts. Immediately drop tablespoonfuls of candy in mounds on prepared baking sheets. Store in refrigerator in airtight container between layers of waxed paper or freeze up to 3 months.

Makes about 3 dozen pieces

Stuffed Pecans

▌▌▌

½ cup semisweet chocolate chips
¼ cup sweetened condensed milk
½ teaspoon vanilla
Powdered sugar (about ½ cup)
80 large pecan halves

Melt chips in small saucepan over very low heat, stirring constantly. Remove from heat. Stir in sweetened condensed milk and vanilla until smooth. Stir in enough sugar to make stiff mixture. Refrigerate, if needed.

Place 1 rounded teaspoonful chocolate mixture on flat side of 1 pecan half. Top with another pecan half. Repeat with remaining pecans and chocolate mixture. Store in refrigerator.

Makes about 40 candies

Easy Luscious Fudge

| | |

2 cups (12 ounces) semisweet chocolate chips
¾ cup milk chocolate chips
2 squares (1 ounce each) unsweetened chocolate, coarsely chopped
1 can (14 ounces) sweetened condensed milk
1 cup mini marshmallows
½ cup chopped walnuts (optional)

Line 8-inch square pan with foil, extending 1-inch over ends of pan. Lightly grease foil.

Melt chocolates in medium saucepan over low heat, stirring constantly. Remove from heat. Stir in condensed milk; add marshmallows and walnuts, if desired, stirring until combined.

Spread chocolate mixture evenly in prepared pan. Score into 2-inch triangles by cutting halfway through fudge with sharp knife while fudge is still warm.

Refrigerate until firm. Remove from pan by lifting fudge and foil. Place on cutting board; cut along score lines into triangles. Remove foil. Store in airtight container in refrigerator.

Makes about 3 dozen pieces

Variation: For Mint Fudge, substitute 1⅔ cups (10 ounces) mint chocolate chips for semisweet chips and ½ cup chopped peppermint candies for walnuts.

Cook's Notes

For a unique holiday flavor substitute pine nuts for walnuts. To bring out a more intense nut flavor, toast and cool the pine nuts before adding them to the recipe.

Butter Toffee Crunch

III

¾ **cup butter or margarine**
1 **tablespoon corn syrup**
 Hot water
1 **cup sugar**
1 **package (2¼ ounces)**
   sliced almonds (about
   ¾ **cup)**

1. Place butter in microwavable 2-quart bowl. Microwave at HIGH 1 minute or until melted.

2. Stir in corn syrup, 2 tablespoons hot water and sugar. Microwave at HIGH 4 minutes, stirring after 1 minute. Add 1 tablespoon hot water; stir to combine. Microwave at HIGH 1 minute.

3. Stir in almonds. Microwave at HIGH 2 to 3 minutes, until light caramel in color.

4. Pour onto an ungreased baking sheet. Spread out candy. Cool until set. Break into pieces. Store in airtight container.
Makes about ¾ pound

Variation: Sprinkle hot candy with 1 cup milk chocolate chips. Let melt; spread.

Tip: If kitchen is cold, warm the baking sheet before pouring out toffee. It will spread more easily and be thinner.

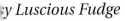
y Luscious Fudge

Eggnog Gift Fudge

▮▮▮

INGREDIENTS
¾ cup prepared eggnog
2 tablespoons light corn syrup
2 tablespoons butter or margarine
2 cups sugar
1 teaspoon vanilla

SUPPLIES
Pastry brush
Candy thermometer
Ribbon bows

1. Butter 8×8-inch pan. Lightly butter inside of heavy, medium saucepan.

2. Combine eggnog, corn syrup, butter and sugar in prepared saucepan. Cook over medium heat, stirring constantly, until sugar dissolves and mixture comes to a boil. Wash down sides of pan with pastry brush frequently dipped in hot water to remove sugar crystals.

3. Add candy thermometer. Continue to cook until mixture reaches 238°F (soft-ball stage).

4. Pour into large heatproof bowl. Cool to lukewarm (about 110°F).

5. Add vanilla; beat with electric mixer until thick.

Spread in prepared pan. Score fudge into 36 squares with knife. Refrigerate until firm. Cut into squares. Wrap in plastic wrap and top with bows as shown in photo (page 75).

Makes 3 dozen pieces

White Chocolate-Dipped Apricots

▮▮▮

3 ounces white chocolate, coarsely chopped
20 dried apricot halves

Line baking sheet with waxed paper; set aside. Melt white chocolate in bowl over hot (not boiling) water; stir constantly.

Dip half of each apricot piece in chocolate, coating both sides. Place on prepared baking sheet. Refrigerate until firm. Store in refrigerator in container between layers of waxed paper.

Makes 20 apricots

White Chocolate-Dipped Apricots and Stuffed Pecans (page 68)

Cherry Merry Christmas Crunch

▌▌▌

2 cups walnut halves
1 cup candied red and green
    cherries, cut in half
2 tablespoons butter or
    margarine
1 teaspoon salt
1 teaspoon maple extract
¼ teaspoon cherry extract
2 cups sugar
¾ cup light corn syrup
¼ cup maple syrup

Generously grease baking
sheet; set aside.

Combine walnuts, cherries,
butter, salt and extracts in
medium bowl; set aside.
Combine sugar, corn syrup
and maple syrup in heavy,
large saucepan. Bring to a boil.
Carefully clip candy
thermometer to side of pan
(do not let bulb touch bottom
of pan). Cook over medium
heat until thermometer
registers 300°F (hard-crack
stage). Remove from heat; stir
in walnut mixture. Quickly
pour onto prepared baking
sheet. Cool completely. Break
into pieces.
   Makes about 2 pounds candy

Chocolate Peppermints

▌▌▌

1 cup (6 ounces) semisweet
    chocolate chips
1 cup (6 ounces) milk
    chocolate chips
¼ teaspoon peppermint
    extract
½ cup crushed peppermint
    candy

Line baking sheet with
buttered waxed paper; set
aside. Melt both kinds of chips
in heavy, medium saucepan
over low heat, stirring
constantly. Stir in peppermint
extract. Spread mixture in
rectangle about ¼ inch thick
on prepared baking sheet.
Sprinkle with candy; press into
chocolate. Refrigerate until
almost firm. Cut into squares.*
Refrigerate until firm before
removing from paper.
   Makes about 100 mints

*Squares are easier to cut without
breaking if chocolate is not completely
firm.*

*Top to bottom: Cherry Merry
Christmas Crunch and
Eggnog Gift Fudge (page 72)*

Double-Decker Fudge

∎ ∎ ∎

1 cup REESE'S® Peanut Butter Chips
1 cup HERSHEY'S Semi-Sweet Chocolate Chips or HERSHEY'S MINI CHIPS™ Semi-Sweet Chocolate
2¼ cups sugar
1 jar (7 ounces) marshmallow creme
¾ cup evaporated milk
¼ cup (½ stick) butter
1 teaspoon vanilla extract

1. Line 8-inch square pan with foil, extending foil over edges of pan. Measure peanut butter chips into one medium bowl and chocolate chips into a second medium bowl.

2. Combine sugar, marshmallow creme, evaporated milk and butter in heavy 3-quart saucepan. Cook over medium heat, stirring constantly, until mixture boils; boil and stir 5 minutes. Remove from heat; stir in vanilla. Immediately stir one-half of the hot mixture (1½ cups) into peanut butter chips until chips are completely melted; quickly pour into prepared pan. Stir remaining one-half hot mixture into chocolate chips until chips are completely melted. Quickly spread over top of peanut butter layer.

3. Cool completely. Remove from pan; place on cutting board. Peel off and discard foil; cut into 1-inch squares. Store tightly covered.
Makes about 5 dozen pieces or about 2 pounds candy

PEANUT BUTTER FUDGE: Omit chocolate chips; place 1⅔ cups (10-ounce package) REESE'S® Peanut Butter Chips in large bowl. Cook fudge mixture as directed. Add to chips; stir until chips are completely melted. Pour into prepared pan; cool.

CHOCOLATE FUDGE: Omit peanut butter chips; place 2 cups (12-ounce package) HERSHEY'S Semi-Sweet Chocolate Chips or HERSHEY'S MINICHIPS® Semi-Sweet Chocolate in large bowl. Cook fudge mixture as directed above; add to chips; stir until chips are completely melted. Pour into prepared pan; cool.

Note: For best results, do not double this recipe.

Top to bottom: Rich Cocoa Fudge (page 78) and Double Decker Fudge

Rich Cocoa Fudge

▍▍▍

3 cups sugar
⅔ cup HERSHEY'S Cocoa or
HERSHEY'S Dutch
Processed Cocoa
⅛ teaspoon salt
1½ cups milk
¼ cup (½ stick) butter
1 teaspoon vanilla extract

1. Line 8- or 9-inch square pan with foil, extending foil over edges of pan. Butter foil.

2. Stir together sugar, cocoa and salt in heavy 4-quart saucepan; stir in milk. Cook over medium heat, stirring constantly, until mixture comes to full rolling boil. Boil, without stirring, until mixture reaches 234°F on candy thermometer, or until small amount of mixture dropped into very cold water forms a soft ball which flattens when removed from water. (Bulb of candy thermometer should not rest on bottom of saucepan.) Remove from heat.

3. Add butter and vanilla. DO NOT STIR. Cool at room temperature to 110°F (lukewarm). Beat with wooden spoon until fudge thickens and just begins to lose some of its gloss. Quickly spread into prepared pan; cool completely. Cut into squares. Store in tightly covered container at room temperature.

Makes about 3 dozen pieces or 1¾ pounds

Note: For best results, do not double this recipe.

Nutty Rich Cocoa Fudge: Beat cooked fudge as directed. Immediately stir in 1 cup chopped almonds, pecans or walnuts and quickly spread into prepared pan.

Marshmallow Nut Cocoa Fudge: Increase cocoa to ¾ cup. Cook fudge as directed. Add 1 cup marshmallow creme with butter and vanilla. DO NOT STIR. Cool to 110°F (lukewarm). Beat 8 minutes; stir in 1 cup chopped nuts. Pour into prepared pan. (Fudge does not set until poured into pan.)

Prep Time: 25 minutes
Cook Time: 25 minutes
Cool Time: 2½ hours

Festive Popcorn Treats

▌▌▌

6 cups popped popcorn
½ cup sugar
½ cup light corn syrup
¼ cup peanut butter
    Green food color
¼ cup red cinnamon candies

Line baking sheet with waxed paper. Pour popcorn into large bowl. Combine sugar and corn syrup in medium saucepan. Bring to a boil over medium heat, stirring constantly; boil 1 minute. Remove from heat. Add peanut butter and green food color; stir until peanut butter is completely melted. Pour over popcorn; stir to coat well. Lightly butter hands and shape popcorn mixture into pine tree shapes. While trees are still warm, press red cinnamon candies into trees. Place on prepared baking sheet; let stand until firm, about 30 minutes.

Makes 6 servings

Tiger Stripes

▌▌▌

1 package (12 ounces) semisweet chocolate chips
3 tablespoons chunky peanut butter, divided
2 (2-ounce) white chocolate baking bars

Line 8-inch square pan with foil. Grease lightly. Melt semisweet chocolate and 2 tablespoons peanut butter in small saucepan over low heat; stir well. Pour half of chocolate mixture into prepared pan. Let stand 10 to 15 minutes to cool slightly. Melt white baking bars with remaining 1 tablespoon peanut butter over low heat in small saucepan. Spoon half of white chocolate mixture over dark chocolate mixture. Drop remaining dark and white chocolate mixtures by spoonfuls over mixture in pan. Using small metal spatula or knife, pull through the chocolates to create tiger stripes. Freeze about 1 hour or until firm. Remove from pan; peel off foil. Cut into 36 pieces. Refrigerate until ready to serve.

Makes 3 dozen pieces

3...2...1...
Happy New Year!

Cranberry Sangría

III

1 bottle (750 ml) Beaujolais or dry red wine
1 cup cranberry juice cocktail
1 cup orange juice
½ cup cranberry-flavored liqueur (optional)
1 orange, thinly sliced
1 lime, thinly sliced

Combine wine, cranberry juice cocktail, orange juice, liqueur, orange slices and lime slices in large glass pitcher. Chill 2 to 8 hours before serving.

Pour into glasses; add orange and/or lime slices from sangría to each glass.

Makes about 7 cups, 10 to 12 servings

Sparkling Sangría: Just before serving, tilt pitcher and slowly add 2 cups well-chilled sparkling water or club soda. Pour into glasses; add orange and/or lime slices from sangría to each glass. Makes about 9 cups, 12 to 15 servings.

Antipasto Crescent Bites

▌▌▌

2 ounces cream cheese (do not use reduced-fat or fat-free cream cheese)
1 package (8 ounces) refrigerated crescent roll dough
1 egg *plus* 1 tablespoon water, beaten
4 strips roasted red pepper, cut into 3×¾-inch-long strips
2 large marinated artichoke hearts, cut in half lengthwise to ¾-inch width
1 thin slice Genoa or other salami, cut into 4 strips
4 small stuffed green olives, cut in half

1. Preheat oven to 375°F. Cut cream cheese into 16 equal pieces, about 1 teaspoon per piece; set aside.

2. Remove dough from package. Unroll on lightly floured surface. Cut each triangle of dough in half to form 2 triangles. Brush outer edges of triangle lightly with beaten egg.

3. Wrap 1 pepper strip around 1 piece of cream cheese. Place on dough triangle. Fold over and pinch edges to seal; repeat with remaining pepper strips. Place 1 piece artichoke heart and 1 piece of cream cheese on dough triangle. Fold over and pinch edges to seal; repeat with remaining pieces of artichoke hearts. Wrap 1 strip salami around 1 piece of cream cheese. Place on dough triangle. Fold over and pinch edges to seal; repeat with remaining salami. Place 2 olive halves and 1 piece of cream cheese on dough triangle. Fold over and pinch edges to seal; repeat with remaining olives. Place evenly spaced on ungreased baking sheet. Brush with beaten egg.

4. Bake 12 to 14 minutes, or until golden brown. Cool on wire rack. Store in airtight container in refrigerator.

5. Reheat on baking sheet in preheated 325°F oven 7 to 8 minutes or until warmed through. Do not microwave.

Makes 16 pieces

Antipasto Crescent Bites

Deviled Shrimp

▌▌▌

Devil Sauce (recipe
   follows)
2 eggs, lightly beaten
¼ teaspoon salt
¼ teaspoon **TABASCO**® brand
   Pepper Sauce
1 quart vegetable oil
1 pound raw shrimp, peeled
   and cleaned
1 cup dry bread crumbs

Prepare Devil Sauce; set aside.
Stir together eggs, salt and
TABASCO® Sauce in shallow
dish until well blended. Pour
oil into heavy 3-quart
saucepan or deep-fat fryer,
filling no more than ⅓ full.
Heat oil over medium heat to
375°F. Dip shrimp into egg
mixture, then into bread
crumbs; shake off excess.
Carefully add shrimp to oil, a
few at a time. Cook 1 to 2
minutes or until golden. Drain
on paper towels. Just before
serving, drizzle Devil Sauce
over shrimp.

*Makes 6 appetizer
servings*

DEVIL SAUCE

2 tablespoons butter *or*
   margarine
1 small onion, finely chopped
1 clove garlic, minced
1½ teaspoons dry mustard
½ cup beef consommé
2 tablespoons
   Worcestershire sauce
2 tablespoons dry white wine
¼ teaspoon **TABASCO**® brand
   Pepper Sauce
¼ cup lemon juice

Melt butter in 1-quart
saucepan over medium heat;
add onion and garlic. Stirring
frequently, cook 3 minutes or
until tender. Blend in mustard.
Gradually stir in consommé,
Worcestershire sauce, wine
and TABASCO® Sauce until well
blended. Bring to a boil and
simmer 5 minutes. Stir in
lemon juice. Serve warm over
shrimp or use as a dip.

Makes about 1¼ cups

Orange Juice & Champagne

▌▌▌

6 teaspoons orange-flavored liquer
1 quart orange juice, chilled
1 bottle (750 ml) champagne, chilled
Strawberries for garnish

Pour 1 teaspoon liqueur into each of 6 wine glasses. Fill each glass two-thirds full with orange juice. Fill glasses with champagne. Garnish, if desired. Serve immediately.

Makes 6 servings

Serve It With Style!

This refreshing drink is also known as a Mimosa. It has long been a favorite for holiday brunches. Garnish it with a sugar cube or maraschino cherry, if you like.

Holiday Meatballs

▌▌▌

1½ pounds lean ground beef
⅔ cup dry bread crumbs
1 egg, slightly beaten
¼ cup water
3 tablespoons minced onion
1 clove garlic, minced
½ teaspoon salt
¼ teaspoon pepper
1 tablespoon vegetable oil
1 cup HEINZ® Chili Sauce
1 cup grape jelly

Combine first 8 ingredients. Form into 60 bite-sized meatballs using rounded teaspoon for each. Place in shallow baking pan or jelly roll pan brushed with oil. Bake in 450°F oven 15 minutes or until cooked through. Meanwhile, in small saucepan, combine chili sauce and grape jelly. Heat until jelly is melted. Place well-drained meatballs in serving dish. Pour chili sauce mixture over; stir gently to coat. Serve warm.

Makes 60 appetizers

Tip: For a zestier sauce, substitute hot jalapeño jelly for grape jelly.

Holiday Beef Steaks with Vegetable Sauté and Hot Mustard Sauce

■ ■ ■

Boneless beef top loin
     steaks, cut 1 inch thick
½ cup plain yogurt
1 teaspoon cornstarch
¼ cup condensed beef broth
2 teaspoons coarse-grained
     mustard
1 teaspoon prepared grated
     horseradish
1 teaspoon Dijon-style
     mustard
¼ teaspoon sugar
½ teaspoon lemon-pepper
1 package (16 ounces)
     frozen whole green
     beans
1 cup quartered large
     mushrooms
1 tablespoon butter
¼ cup water

Place yogurt and cornstarch in medium saucepan and stir until blended. Stir in beef broth, coarse-grained mustard, horseradish, Dijon-style mustard and sugar; reserve. Press an equal amount of lemon-pepper into surface of boneless beef top loin steaks. Place steaks on rack in broiler pan so surface of steaks is 3 to 4 inches from heat. Broil steaks 13 to 17 minutes for medium rare to medium doneness, turning once. Meanwhile, cook beans and mushrooms in butter in large frying pan over medium heat 6 minutes, stirring occasionally. Add water; cover and continue cooking 6 to 8 minutes, stirring occasionally until beans are tender. Cook reserved sauce over medium-low heat 5 minutes, stirring until sauce is slightly thickened. Serve steaks and vegetables with sauce.

Makes 6 servings

Note: A boneless beef top loin steak will yield three to four 3-ounce cooked servings per pound.

Prep Time: 15 minutes
Cook Time: 15 minutes

Favorite recipe from **National Cattlemen's Beef Association**

Blue Crab Stuffed Tomatoes

▌▌▌

½ pound Florida blue
   crabmeat
10 plum tomatoes
½ cup finely chopped celery
⅓ cup plain low fat yogurt
2 tablespoons minced green
   onion
2 tablespoons finely chopped
   red bell pepper
½ teaspoon lemon juice
¼ teaspoon salt
⅛ teaspoon black pepper

Remove any shell or cartilage
from crabmeat.

Cut tomatoes in half
lengthwise. Carefully scoop out
centers of tomatoes; discard
pulp. Invert on paper towels.

Combine crabmeat, celery,
yogurt, onion, red pepper,
lemon juice, salt and black
pepper. Mix well.

Fill tomato halves with crab
mixture. Refrigerate 2 hours.
Makes 20 appetizers

Favorite recipe from **Florida
Department of Agriculture
and Consumer Services,
Bureau of Seafood and
Aquaculture**

Ginger Pineapple Mold

▌▌▌

1 can (20 ounces) crushed
   pineapple in juice,
   undrained
1½ cups boiling water
1 package (8-serving size) or
   2 packages (4-serving
   size) JELL-O® Brand Lime
   Flavor Gelatin Dessert
1 cup cold ginger ale or
   water
¼ teaspoon ground ginger

DRAIN pineapple, reserving
juice. Stir boiling water into
gelatin in large bowl at least
2 minutes until completely
dissolved. Stir in reserved
juice, ginger ale and ginger.
Refrigerate about 1¼ hours
or until slightly thickened
(consistency of unbeaten egg
whites).

STIR in pineapple. Pour into
5-cup mold.

REFRIGERATE 4 hours or until
firm. Unmold.
Makes 10 servings

Preparation Time: 20 minutes
Refrigerating Time: 5¼ hours

Raspberry Wine Punch

▌▌▌

1 package (10 ounces) frozen red raspberries in syrup, thawed
1 bottle (750 ml) white Zinfandel or blush wine
¼ cup raspberry-flavored liqueur
Empty ½ gallon milk or juice carton
3 to 4 cups distilled water, divided
Sprigs of pine and tinsel
Fresh cranberries

Process raspberries with syrup in food processor or blender until smooth; press through strainer, discarding seeds. Combine wine, raspberry purée and liqueur in pitcher; refrigerate until serving time. Rinse out wine bottle and remove label.

Fully open top of carton. Place wine bottle in center of carton. Tape bottle securely to carton so bottle will not move when adding water. Pour 2 cups distilled water into carton. Carefully push pine sprigs, cranberries and tinsel into water between bottle and carton to form decorative design. Add remaining water to almost fill carton. Freeze until firm, 8 hours or overnight.

Just before serving, peel carton from ice block. Using funnel, pour punch back into wine bottle. Wrap bottom of ice block with white cotton napkin or towel to hold while serving.

Makes 8 servings

Note: Punch may also be served in punch bowl, if desired.

New Year's Day Black-Eyed Peas

▌▌▌

½ pound dried black-eyed peas, sorted and rinsed
4 cups water
1 small onion, chopped
1 clove garlic, minced
½ teaspoon pepper
1 large bay leaf
⅛ teaspoon dried thyme leaves, crushed
⅓ cup FILIPPO BERIO® Extra Virgin Olive Oil
2 tablespoons wine vinegar
Hot cooked rice (optional)

1. Place peas and water in medium saucepan; bring to a boil over high heat.

2. Reduce heat; stir in onion, garlic, pepper, bay leaf, thyme, olive oil and vinegar. Cover; simmer 1 hour or until peas are tender. Drain peas; remove and discard bay leaf. Serve with rice, if desired.

Makes 4 servings

Variation: For cold salad, prepare peas as directed in step 1. Stir in only the bay leaf; cover and simmer 1 hour or until peas are tender. Drain peas; remove and discard bay leaf. Add onion, garlic, pepper and thyme. In small bowl, whisk together olive oil and vinegar. Pour over pea mixture; stir to combine. Cover; refrigerate at least 2 hours before serving.

Prep Time: 10 minutes
Cook Time: 1 hour
Chill Time: 2 hours (salad only)

Cook's Nook

It has long been a southern tradition to serve black-eyed peas on New Year's Day. They are said to bring good luck and prosperity for the new year.

Raspberry Wine Punch

Peppered Beef Tip Roast with Corn Pudding

❚❚❚

1 (3½- to 5-pound) beef tip roast
2 teaspoons black pepper
2 teaspoons dry mustard
½ teaspoon ground allspice
½ teaspoon ground red pepper
1 large clove garlic, minced
1 teaspoon vegetable oil
Corn Pudding (recipe follows)

Preheat oven to 325°F. Combine black pepper, mustard, allspice, ground red pepper and garlic; stir in oil to form paste.

Spread mixture evenly on surface of beef tip roast. Place roast, fat side up, on rack in open roasting pan. Insert meat thermometer into thickest part of roast. Roast until thermometer registers 155°F for medium or until desired doneness, allowing 30 to 35 minutes per pound. Meanwhile prepare Corn Pudding. Allow roast to stand 15 to 20 minutes before carving. *Do not add water. Do not cover.* Meanwhile, prepare Corn Pudding. Allow roast to stand 15 to 20 minutes before carving. Roast will rise about 5°F in temperature to reach 160°F. Serve carved roast with Corn Pudding.

Makes 2 to 4 servings per pound

CORN PUDDING

1 bag (20 ounces) frozen whole kernel corn, thawed
1 small onion, quartered
2 cups milk
2 eggs, beaten
1 package (8½ ounces) corn muffin mix
½ teaspoon salt
1 cup shredded Cheddar cheese
1 cup thinly sliced romaine lettuce
½ cup julienned radishes

Preheat oven to 325°F. Combine corn and onion in food processor; cover and process using on/off pulse until corn is broken but not puréed, scraping side of bowl as necessary. Add milk and eggs; pulse until just blended. Add muffin mix and salt; pulse only until mixed. Pour mixture into greased 11¾×7½-inch baking dish. Bake 45 to 50 minutes or until outside crust is golden brown. Sprinkle pudding with cheese; place under broiler 3 to 4 inches from heat. Broil until cheese is melted and top is crusty. To serve, top with romain lettuce and radishes.

Makes 8 to 10 servings

Favorite recipe from **National Cattlemen's Beef Association**

Peppered Beef Tip Roast

ACKNOWLEDGMENTS

The publishers would like to thank the companies and organizations listed below for the use of their recipes and photographs in this publication.

Almond Board of California

Bestfoods

Blue Diamond Growers®

Bob Evans®

Campbell Soup Company

Dole Food Company, Inc.

Duncan Hines® and Moist Deluxe® are registered trademarks of Aurora Foods Inc.

Filippo Berio Olive Oil

Florida Department of Agriculture and Consumer Services, Bureau of Seafood and Aquaculture

Hebrew National®

Heinz U.S.A.

Hershey Foods Corporation

Kraft Foods, Inc.

Land O' Lakes, Inc.

Lawry's® Foods, Inc.

Lipton®

McIlhenny Company (TABASCO® brand Pepper Sauce)

National Cattlemen's Beef Association

Perdue Farms Incorporated

Reckitt & Colman Inc.

Riviana Foods Inc.

The Procter & Gamble Company

The J.M. Smucker Company

Washington Apple Commission

INDEX